D

Famous Artists

Get to Know
Andy
Warhol

Charlotte Taylor

Enslow Publishing
101 W. 23rd Street
Suite 240
New York, NY 10011
USA

enslow.com

Published in 2016 by Enslow Publishing, LLC
101 W. 23rd Street, Suite 240, New York, NY 10011

Library of Congress Cataloging-in-Publication Data

Taylor, Charlotte, 1978- author.
 Get to know Andy Warhol / Charlotte Taylor.
    pages cm. — (Famous artists)
 Includes bibliographical information and index.
 Summary: "Describes the life and work of artist Andy Warhol"— Provided by publisher.
 ISBN 978-0-7660-7218-3 (library binding)
 ISBN 978-0-7660-7216-9 (pbk)
 ISBN 978-0-7660- 7217-6 (6pk)
 1. Warhol, Andy, 1928-1987—Juvenile literature. 2. Artists—United States—Biography—Juvenile
literature. I. Title.
 N6537.W28T39 2016
 700.92—dc23
 [B]

                                   2015026939

Printed in the United States of America

To Our Readers: We have done our best to make sure all website addresses in this book were
active and appropriate when we went to press. However, the author and the publisher have no
control over and assume no liability for the material available on those websites or any websites
they may link to. Any comments or suggestions can be sent by e-mail to customerservice@enslow.
com.

Portions of this book originally appeared in the book *Andy Warhol: The Life of an Artist* by Carin T.
Ford.

Contents

Andy Warhol grew up in Pittsburgh, Pennsylvania, in a working-class neighborhood.

Chapter 1

Young Andy

When Andy Warhola was four years old, he went to school for the first time. A girl hit him and made him cry. Andy decided that he did not like school.

Andy's brother Paul had made him go to school. Paul was the head of the family whenever their father had to travel. Andy told his mother he did not want to go back to school.

Andy's mother decided to keep him home. She enjoyed drawing. For the next two years, Andy and his mother spent many hours together drawing pictures.

Andy would draw and paint pictures for the rest of his life. He liked painting pictures of things people saw every day, in their homes, and on supermarket shelves. His paintings included dollar bills, Coca-Cola bottles, and Campbell's soup cans.

This kind of art is called Pop Art. It was very different from any kind of art people had seen before. It was familiar; people could easily understand it. For this reason, Pop Art established itself more quickly than any other movement in art history.

Still, many people were confused by Andy's work. Some called him a genius . . . others called him a joke.

But Andy—who dropped the final *a* from his last name to make it Warhol—soon became one of the most famous artists in the world. He was known as the Prince of Pop.

The facts about Andy's life are uncertain, and that is the way he liked it.

"I never give my background," he once said, "and anyway, I make it all up differently every time I'm asked."

Art Smarts

Pop Art had its start in England in the 1950s. Using objects and images that were familiar to everyone, it showed that art did not have to be only for very educated people. Anyone could enjoy it.

Early Days

Some facts are known. Andy was born on August 6, 1928, in Pittsburgh, Pennsylvania. He had two older brothers: Paul, born in 1922, and John, born in 1925.

Andy's parents, Julia and Andrei Warhola, were immigrants. They had left Czechoslovakia in search of a better life in the United States.

When Andy was six, he went back to school. He was a quiet and pale child. He looked sickly. Andy would do his homework after school. Then, he would spend the rest of the afternoon drawing pictures.

Andy became sick with an illness called Saint Vitus' dance when he was eight. The illness made his arms, legs, and face shake. He could not write, speak clearly, or even tie his shoes.

Again, he was kept home with his mother. Julia Warhola bought him comic books, movie magazines, and coloring books. Whenever Andy finished a page in his coloring book, Julia gave him a candy bar. Eventually, he got well.

Andy grew to like drawing portraits of his neighbors and cousins. Soon he was taking free art classes at Pittsburgh's Carnegie Museum of Art. One of his teachers said, "A more talented person than Andy Warhol I never knew."

Andy's first "painting," 1937

Young Andy is pictured here next to his first painting, completed in 1937.

Chapter 2

An Unusual Student

Andy spent all of his free time drawing pictures. Often, his mother had to bring his dinner up to his room because Andy was too busy drawing to come down for meals.

Shortly before Andy entered high school, his father died. Andrei Warhola had come down with hepatitis, a disease that harms the liver. He had hoped that Andy would be well educated. To make sure of that, he had put some money aside.

At Schenley High School, Andy continued to draw. He carried his sketchbook with him everywhere.

When Andy was close to graduating from high school, he was accepted at both the Carnegie Institute of Technology and the University of Pittsburgh. The money Andrei Warhola had set aside

to
Tony
Curtis

andy Warhol

The Some Like it Hot
Shoe

One of Warhol's early jobs was doing the illustrations for a shoe company. This particular drawing hints to his future paintings of Marylin Monroe. *Some Like It Hot* was one of her more popular films.

would pay for his son's college classes. Andy chose Carnegie because it had the better art department.

A Genius or a Fake?

Andy attracted attention as soon as he entered college. The teachers in the art department could not decide whether Warhol was wonderfully talented or had no ability to draw at all. This question is still asked today. That is the mystery of Andy Warhol: Was he a genius or did he just fool people into thinking he was? "If anyone had asked me at the time who was the least likely to succeed, I would have said Andy Warhola," said Robert Lepper, an art teacher at the college.

Warhol was extremely quiet; he almost never spoke. He walked around the campus in baggy blue jeans, a ragged shirt, and torn sneakers.

Often, his art projects had nothing to do with what the teacher had assigned. Sometimes, he handed in ripped pieces of construction paper held together with tape. He even turned in papers that were covered with paw prints from his cat.

By the end of Warhol's first year of college, he was told he must repeat a class he had failed. He also needed to turn in several art projects by the end of summer or he would have to leave school.

Warhol worked hard that summer. He sold fruits and vegetables from his brother Paul's truck every day. While he

Both as an art student and a professional artist, Warhol stood out thanks to his unique style and view of life.

worked, Warhol drew the people he saw: mothers holding babies, women in ragged clothing.

The sketches were so good that they were displayed in the school. Warhol even won a prize of $40 (about $300 today). Most important, he was allowed to continue college.

Chapter 3

"I Can Draw Anything"

After college, Warhol knew he wanted to get a job as an artist. He decided to move to New York City. So, he stuffed his paintings and drawings into a brown paper bag and headed north in 1949.

He had an interview at *Glamour* magazine with editor Tina Fredericks. She was especially impressed by Warhol's style of drawing. He would draw a picture in ink on a piece of paper. Then, he would press this paper down onto a clean sheet of paper and rub hard. The rubbed drawing had a broken-up, or blotted, look to it because not all of the ink transferred evenly.

Fredericks wanted to know if Warhol could draw pictures of practical things, such as clothing and shoes.

"I can draw anything," Warhol said.

He was hired.

Soon, several other magazines gave Warhol work. He also illustrated record album covers, greeting cards, and book jackets.

Raggedy Andy

At that time, most young men trying to get jobs in advertising made sure to dress very nicely. But Warhol wore baggy cotton pants, T-shirts, and sneakers. He carried his work in a brown paper bag. During one visit with a magazine editor, a cockroach crawled out of his bag. The editor felt sorry for Warhol and hired him. His friends nicknamed him Raggedy Andy and Andy Paperbag.

Warhol preferred to work through the night and sleep during the day. This was a habit he would continue throughout his lifetime. It was not just because he enjoyed the quiet of night. He was actually afraid of the dark and preferred staying awake.

The amount of time Warhol spent drawing was hard on his eyes. Soon, he began wearing thick glasses.

Start of Success

All through the 1950s, Warhol worked hard as a commercial artist—someone who draws illustrations that help sell products.

This photo, taken in 1964, shows Warhol with his mother. The two maintained a close relationship over the years.

His name became well known throughout New York City. He earned a lot of money and won many prizes.

But Warhol wanted more.

He once told a friend he wanted to be as famous as the Queen of England. Warhol knew that commercial artists did not usually become famous. But serious artists could.

So he asked his friend, interior designer Muriel Latow, what he could paint that would make people notice him. She told him to paint things that people saw every day at home and in stores. "Something like a can of Campbell's soup," she said.

Warhol liked the idea. He told his mother, who now lived with him in New York, to go to the supermarket. He wanted her to buy every kind of Campbell's soup.

And when he was surrounded by all thirty-two varieties of soup, Warhol began to paint.

Painting soup cans is what made Warhol famous. These limited edition labels on Campbell's soups were inspired by his paintings. They were released in October 2013.

Chapter 4

Soup Cans and Soda Bottles

Warhol made many different paintings of the soup cans. He like to experiment as he painted. Sometimes the soup cans were very large; other times they were small. Sometimes one soup can filled the entire canvas; other times one hundred cans were in a single painting.

Warhol's paintings were put on sale at a gallery in Los Angeles, California. People were puzzled and amused by his work. Soon, he became known throughout the world as the artist who painted Campbell's soup cans.

Warhol's paintings went on display at other galleries. There were pictures of dollar bills, Coca-Cola bottles, movie stars (such as Marilyn Monroe), and, of course, the soup cans.

Coca Cola [4] (1962, Private Collection). In 2010, this painting sold at an auction for $35.36 million.

Warhol created a sculpture made of one hundred boxes of Brillo pads. Brillo pads are a common product used to clean pots and pans.

By the early 1960s, he was considered one of the country's top Pop artists. Warhol caught the public's attention not only because of his artwork but also because of who he was. He became famous for the way he dressed and the way he spoke. The public seemed to be forever interested in what Warhol would do next.

Disaster Art

Using a process called silk-screening, Warhol began painting pictures of disasters: plane and car crashes, funerals, and suicides. He based his silk screens on newspaper photographs. Often, he repeated one picture over and over on the same canvas, just as he had with the soup cans. He had surprised people with his soup cans, but he shocked them now with his disaster paintings. Warhol was trying to show that anything will begin to feel less shocking—even a horrible car crash—if you look at it over and over again.

Warhol next decided to try sculpture. He used his silk-screening process on wooden crates. He made hundreds of boxes of Campbell's tomato juice, Kellogg's corn flakes, Del Monte peaches, Mott's apple juice, and Brillo pads.

By this time, Warhol had a huge studio to work in. He named it the Factory. He chose this name because he knew

Art Smarts

Warhol's silk screens began with a photograph or drawing. Next, he prepared a special piece of silk with the picture and stretched it across a canvas. Then he forced paint through the silk onto the canvas with a rubber roller.

This photo, taken in 1973 shows Warhol standing in front of one of his silkscreens of flowers.

that his system of making art was similar to the way products were made on an assembly line in a factory.

Warhol's Brillo boxes were displayed at a New York gallery in 1964. As always, people were amused and fascinated by his latest creations. But the same question kept turning up about Warhol's work: Was it really art?

Warhol's style created something new: Pop Art was for the average person. From cleaning products to food products to celebrities, Warhol created art that everyone could recognize.

Chapter 5

Making Movies

Being a world-famous artist was not enough for Warhol. Now, he wanted to try making movies.

Warhol still believed that the artist should be removed from his art to make it more real. So, instead of "making" a movie, he often just turned on his camera and let the film roll. The actors could say or do whatever they liked while the film ran.

Sleep was a six-hour film of a man sleeping. *Eat* was a movie in which a man ate a mushroom for forty-five minutes. These films were both silent. Soon, he added music, talking, and color.

Warhol's artwork usually confused people, and so did his movies. Many people thought the films were a waste of time. Others thought Warhol had come up with something new and exciting. But just like Warhol's paintings—which contained any

Warhol's films were as highly debated as his artwork. Here, he is on the set of *Chelsea Girls* at the Factory in 1966.

drips and splashes he made—his movies tried to show what real life was like.

Celebrity Life

As always, Warhol drew attention wherever he went. He now dressed all in black and wore boots, dark glasses, and a silver wig. Andy was very concerned about his weight and often took diet pills to stay thin. The pills also kept him from sleeping very much. He said that from 1965 until 1967, he slept only two or three hours a night.

Warhol did not speak much. One magazine editor said all she ever heard from him were such comments as, "Gee," "Wow," "Really?" "Oh," "Ah," and "Er."

The Factory also drew attention. Everything in the studio was covered with silver paint or aluminum foil. The floor, the ceiling, the furniture, even the cabinets were silver. Millionaires, artists, and actors liked to hang out there.

While he was making movies, Warhol continued to paint. A friend advised him to stop painting disasters and work on something happier. Warhol took the advice and painted hibiscus flowers. He produced hundreds of these paintings. All of them were sold.

Warhol also opened a discotheque (dance club) in New York. The club, called the Dom, was a huge success. It had

Warhol's peculiar behavior only made him a bigger celebrity.

lights flashing on the dance floor, while five movie projectors showed Warhol's films in the background. The rock group the Velvet Underground performed, and a huge mirrored ball hung from the ceiling.

"He became famous in every field he entered," said Tina Fredericks of *Glamour* magazine. "Even though most people are not sure exactly what Andy was famous for."

Warhol was about to become even more famous, but in a way he never could have imagined.

A Shocking Attack

On June 3, 1968, a thirty-two-year-old writer named Valerie Solanas walked into the Factory. She had appeared in one of Warhol's movies. She pulled a gun out of a brown paper bag and shot him in the chest.

Warhol was rushed to the hospital. Although he was pronounced dead, doctors operated on him for more than five hours. He managed to survive.

Warhol stayed in the hospital for six weeks. He thought the gifts he was given of cakes and candies might be poisoned. He asked his nephews to try the food before he would eat it himself.

One of Warhol's paintings of a dollar sign sold for $420 thousand dollars at an auction in July 2015. His paintings are some of the most sought-after and expensive in the world.

Solanas was sentenced to three years in prison. By the end of July, Warhol was able to leave the hospital. "Since I was shot, everything is such a dream to me," he said.

But one thing was definitely not a dream. Since the shooting, the value of Warhol's paintings had skyrocketed. Paintings that once cost a few hundred dollars now cost many thousands.

This front page photo from June 4, 1968, shows Solanas being escorted from the Factory after she shot Warhol.

Chapter 6

Money and Fame

After the shooting, Warhol became even more famous. He was treated like a celebrity wherever he went.

His assistants at the Factory decided this was a good time to have a show of Warhol's work. It would include his various series: the soup cans, Brillo boxes, disaster and flower paintings, and portraits. The show would be held in the United States as well as Europe.

The day after the show opened, in 1971 in Pasadena, California, one of Warhol's paintings was sold at Parke-Bernet, a New York auction house, for $60,000. No living American artist had ever been paid more at auction for his artwork.

This photo, taken in London in 1978, shows Warhol standing in front of his paintings of boxer Muhammad Ali.

Famous Faces

Warhol now spent most of his time painting portraits. One of his most popular subjects was China's Communist leader, Mao Tse-tung. In 1973, Warhol painted two thousand pictures of Mao. The pictures ranged in size from six inches to seventeen feet. Some were done on regular canvas, while others were used as wallpaper rolls.

Warhol decided to start a magazine, called *Interview*, which focused on entertainment and fashion. It set the tone for the celebrity magazines that became popular in the 1980s.

Warhol was very busy dividing his time among painting, making films, and publishing a magazine. He worked every day and made a lot of money. But he was always afraid of being poor. He kept a great deal of money stuffed under his mattress, which was made of straw just for him. Warhol also disliked carrying credit cards. Instead, he walked around with a brown envelope that had several one hundred dollar bills in it.

Collecting Treasures

Warhol enjoyed spending his money and went shopping every day. He considered shopping part of his work. The treasures in his house were worth millions of dollars.

He had many collections: artwork by Pablo Picasso, rare books, bronze statues of horses and dancers, antique furniture,

Mao (1973). Warhol did several paintings of China's Chairman Mao that are now in museums around the world. This one is in the Hamburger Bahnhof Museum of Contemporary Art in Berlin, Germany.

Art Smarts

Warhol loved Hollywood and celebrities. He chose the biggest stars of his time for his portraits. He repeated their image on the canvas over and over. This was his way of showing that celebrities belonged to everyone.

and cookie jars. But Warhol did not like to show off his treasures. In fact, he kept most of the rooms in his house locked.

"He had a routine," said assistant Jed Johnson. "He'd walk through the house every morning before he left, open the door of each room with a key, peer in, then re-lock it. Then, at night when he came home, he would unlock each door, turn the light on, peer in, lock up, and go to bed."

Warhol poses in 1975 with a few special items
that he collected over the years.

Chapter 7

Later Years

As the years went by, Warhol continued to work hard. He hated taking vacations and was never able to relax. If he was not shopping or walking his two dogs, Archie and Amos, Warhol was working on a project.

In the mid-1970s, Warhol was invited to dinner at the White House by President Gerald Ford. Warhol was very nervous. He wore a white tie and formal dinner jacket. He put on blue jeans underneath his dress pants because they were itchy. He also dyed one of his eyebrows white and the other black, and he wore one of his wigs. Warhol would also meet Jimmy Carter just before he was elected president.

From Books to Television

Warhol published a book in 1975 about his thoughts on life. *The Philosophy of Andy Warhol (From A to B and Back Again)* was

Warhol stands next to *Jimmy Carter 76* at a reception on Capitol Hill on June 14, 1977.

based on tapes of Warhol's telephone conversations. He talked about lots of things, including fame, beauty, and death.

The first major show in many years of Warhol's artwork was held in 1977. Andy had painted the symbol of the Communist party, the hammer and sickle. He used silk screens as well as a large sponge mop to apply the paint in broad strokes.

Warhol began working on an idea for a television show. It was thirty minutes long and included talks with people who were wealthy and famous. *Andy Warhol's TV* ran for nine years. The show seemed to lead the way for the music videos that became popular in the 1980s.

Warhol continued painting. Fifty of his portraits were put on display at the Whitney Museum in New York City. Many art critics did not like the show. They called it boring. One critic said the paintings were awful. "He's right," commented Warhol.

Warhol came out with another book, *POPism*. In the book, he wrote about his view of popular culture in New York. In 1985 he traveled to California and appeared in an episode of the television show *The Love Boat*. He also filmed a commercial for Diet Pepsi.

Last Days

Warhol was rich and he was famous. But his nephew George said, "I don't think Uncle Andy was very happy at all, even with all that money and fame."

Warhol traveled to Milan, Italy, in 1987 to attend a show of his version of *The Last Supper.* Italian Renaissance painter Leonardo da Vinci had painted the original masterpiece. Warhol had taken the religious work and redone it in his own style, using advertising logos, such as those of General Electric and Dove soap. Although many people came to the opening, Warhol was not able to enjoy it.

He was in a lot of pain because of an infected gallbladder. When he returned to New York, he was operated on immediately. The surgery went smoothly. But the following morning, February 22, 1987, Warhol died of a heart attack. It is unclear why he had the heart attack and whether it was connected to his medical care.

Starting with his paintings of Campbell's soup cans, Andy Warhol brought Pop Art into people's lives throughout the world. He experimented with sculpture, movies, television, magazines, and music.

Many people consider Andy Warhol the most important American artist of our time. But Warhol once said he only wanted to be remembered as a can of soup.

This photo, taken in 1986, shortly before his death, shows that Warhol never wanted to stop working.

Warhol's *Liz #1* sold for $20,325,000 at a Sotheby's auction in 2013. His work continues to increase in value and is some of the most recognized in the world.

Timeline

1928—Andy Warhola is born on August 6 in Pittsburgh, Pennsylvania.

1945—Warhol enters Carnegie Institute of Technology.

1949—Warhol begins work as a commercial artist in New York City.

1952—Warhol has first gallery opening.

1962—Warhol displays paintings of Campbell's soup cans.

1963—Warhol begins making films.

1968—Warhol is shot by Valerie Solanas.

1969—Warhol publishes *Interview* magazine.

1971—Warhol's work is shown at the Pasadena Museum.

1975—*The Philosophy of Andy Warhol (From A to B and Back Again)* is published.

1977—Warhol's first major show of new work in ten years features hammer-and-sickle paintings.

1986—Warhol opens show of self-portraits in London.

1987—Warhol dies of a heart attack on February 22 after gallbladder surgery.

1994—The Andy Warhol Museum opens in Pittsburgh.

2002—The US Postal Service issues a stamp with Warhol's image.

2015—The Museum of Modern Art in New York City opens a new exhibition of Warhol's work.

Words to Know

canvas—A heavy, specially prepared piece of cloth on which an artist paints.

commercial art—Artwork that is aimed at selling a product, such as a newspaper illustration that advertises shoes.

discotheque—Nightclub where people dance.

gallery—A room or building where artwork is displayed and sold.

immigrant—Person who moves to another country, usually in search of a better life.

logo—Symbol or drawing that people identify with a product, such as the Nike "swoosh."

masterpiece—Artist's work that is generally considered one of the best of its type.

Pop Art—Style of art in which everyday objects, such as soda bottles and lightbulbs, were painted or sculpted.

popular culture—Fashions, books, movies, products, and other things enjoyed by ordinary people.

silk-screening—Process using a specially treated piece of silk stretched across a canvas. It works somewhat like a stencil. An artist can make the same exact design over and over again.

Learn More

Books

Alexander, Heather. *A Child's Introduction to Art: The World's Greatest Paintings and Sculptures.* New York: Black Dog & Leventhal, 2014.

Anderson, Kirsten. *Who Was Andy Warhol?* New York: Grosset & Dunlap, 2014.

Krull, Kathleen. *Lives of the Artists: Masterpieces, Messes (And What the Neighbors Thought).* Boston: Houghton Mifflin Harcourt, 2014.

Temple, Kathryn. *Art for Kids: Drawing.* New York: Sterling, 2014.

Web Sites

The Andy Warhol Museum
http://www.warhol.org
Learn about the artist and view his works in the museum's online collection.

Artcyclopedia, the Fine Art Search Engine: Andy Warhol
http://www.artcyclopedia.com/artists/warhol_andy.html
Contains links to many of Warhol's works as well as biographies and articles.

Art Projects for Kids: Andy Warhol
artprojectsforkids.org/category/view-by-artist/artist-andy-warhol/
Provides ideas for art projects inspired by Warhol's famous paintings.

Index